The Pig Behind The Door

Diane Allan

One Printers Way
Altona, MB R0G0B0,
Canada

www.friesenpress.com

Copyright © 2021 by Diane Allan
First Edition — 2021

All rights reserved.

ISBN
978-1-03-912748-7 (Hardcover)
978-1-03-912747-0 (Paperback)
978-1-03-912749-4 (eBook)

1. POETRY, SUBJECTS & THEMES, NATURE

Distributed to the trade by The Ingram Book Company

The Garden Door

This is how it all began,
a cottage in a wonderland.
An old door faded over time,
windows broken, covered in grime.
An antique doorknob, turn and see
the garden cottage fantasy.
Behind the door, so much more,
a mystery full of garden lore.

Diane Allan

Slum Lord

A slumlord am I, though I would like
to deny,
I am keeping my birds rather grotty.
Though the neighborhood's swell,
and the birdies are well,
it is not for the rich or the snotty.
Collapsing yes, the houses past their best,
the rent is free for the asking.
Though not in a tree, just leave them be,
They are not up for renos or trashing.

My Gardener

My gardener,
sits with me under the tree
sipping wine or maybe tea
planning and dreaming of what could be
or just maintaining reality.
We work together you can see
to make it a possibility
to build this garden for you and me.

The Bay Tree

To think that I should ever see
a poem as lovely as a tree.
A tree that started in a pot
and grew up past the chimney top.
A tree whose leaves you used in stew.
A tree whose leaves were all askew.
Everywhere those leaves were falling,
all year long they came a calling.
Leaves here and leaves there,
leaves were falling everywhere.

Then one day a Faller came.
No one had to take the blame.
It was decided to take it down.
Thud it went to the ground.
Sun came in like never before,
And things could grow forever more.

The Pond

We made this pond in the garden,
digging the hole and all.
We filled it with plants and goldfish
and admired our efforts with awe.
The next day the plants were all eaten
 and not a fish to be seen.
Seems the wildlife enjoyed our efforts,
the pond was a giant tureen.

The Reader

Sitting on a pile of books
sculptured out of stone,
sits a tiny concrete man
wizened like a gnome.

Reading well into the night
never to be heard,
sitting right beside him
a little concrete bird.

They grace the yard with silence
the reader and the bird,
in each other's quiet company
studying the word!

In The Garden

Old folks in the backyard,
groaning about their aches.
Pulling weeds and sowing seeds.
doing what it takes.

The grass is green, the flowers beautiful,
the garden is something to see.
Resting by the greenhouse,
the old folks with their tea.

Birds

Sweet water, seeds, suet and such,
on a daily basis the work is too much.
I collapse in my chair,
my wallet is bare,
how long can I keep this all going?
The feeders are empty, the seeds are
all gone.
The ground is a mess, poop all around
but the birds are delightful, their songs are
the best.
Forgive my remarks, I have been put to
the test.
The birds make the garden.
They are characters in my play
so, I will set the stage for another song
filled day.

Gilded Cage

I'm only a bird in a gilded cage
Swinging to and fro
I'm made of stone
I'm all alone
Screw it!!

The Piggy Party

From Montreal, Victoria and Mexico
they gather one and all
for fun, for laughter, for gaiety,
always obeying the law.

They are copper, steel and concrete
letting their piggy hair down
for this is a piggy party
did someone say drinks all around?

From one snout to another
hold your curly tails up high,
toast to the piggies at the party,
happiness is one pork pie.

Birdhouse

I am made from wood,
sturdy and strong.
Made by a child,
how could this go wrong?
I live in the greenery,
my door is just right
but I remain empty
morning, noon and night.
I do not want to be lonely,
so, my ad will be sent,
"a home made of love
Birdhouse for rent".

Diane Allan

The Hare

He comes he goes, he is so funny,
not much known about that long-
eared hare.
Here he comes again, that playful bunny,
seeing him twice is extremely rare.

Music and laughter he shares with many,
he lives a whole other life, where
parties abound.
Where does he go to have such plenty?
Down the rabbit hole to the underground.

Diane Allan

The Crying Angel

There is an angel sitting in the yard,
his eyes are full of tears.
No one knows why he is crying,
but he has been doing it for years.
He is a sweet little angel,
though he is so very blue,
I wonder what his story is
no one knows, do you?

The Green House

There sits the green house
moldy and old,
a crack in the glass,
a story untold.
Ivy growing through the glass,
rust on all the latches.
Spider webs in every corner,
dirt and grime in patches.
But Sweet Peas would be nice
and spring will soon be here.
Maybe with a little work,
new life will soon appear.

The Dandelion

I'm misunderstood
if only I could
be the star of everyone's garden.
I'm pretty and bright
is there no chance I might
succeed in horticultural jargon?
They say be cool
but who made the rule
no dandelions in the garden?
It's sad to say
It is this way
My curses I hope you pardon.

The Magic Pathway

A rainbow on the forest floor,
a beautiful thing to see.
Shining in the sun,
it belongs, it's meant to be.

A path of many colours,
glitters, shines and glows,
marbles, stones and diamonds,
Sharp on your bare toes.

Winds it's way through the cedars,
to the sea beyond
so joyful in the darkness,
singing out it's song.

The Hikers

Who are these people
hiking through the garden?
Tiny people in weird attire
strolling through the garden.
Could they be well known fashionistas
swaggering through my garden?
Making a statement, a touch of class,
promenading through the garden!

The Trek Of
The Buddhas

The trek of the Buddhas begins from
above in the high serene mountains full of
peace and love.
Meandering through the bamboo
and ferns,
To meet the flute player with no concerns.
A quiet moment until a Racoon,
runs over everyone like a giant Baboon!

The Security Owls

There are three owls in a row,
the three amigos they be.
Watching the night for intruders,
they are doing their job you see.
When its dark its scary,
and things go bump in the night.
The owls stand guard in the garden,
making everything feel alright.

The Pig Behind
The Door

There is a pig behind the door.
She is much too big to ignore.
There is a pig behind the door.

There is a pig behind the door.
How did she get there, I implore?
The giant pig behind the door.

The pig behind the door,
She wears lipstick, whatever for?
That cute pig behind the door.

That cute pig behind the door,
her name is Elsie and what is more,
I love that pig behind the door.

CPSIA information can be obtained
at www.ICGtesting.com
Printed in the USA
BVHW090730311021
620370BV00002B/3